C000016002

WHITE BELT THINKING

Copyright © 2022, All rights reserved.

ISBN:978-1-9161051-2-6

No part of this book may be used or reproduced in any manner
whatsoever without written permission from the author.
Brief passages may be quoted for the purposes of interviews,
reviews, or press with permission and must be credited.
All characters are fictional.

Every effort has been made to ensure this book is free from
errors or omissions. However, the publisher, the author, the
editor, or their respective employees or agents, shall not accept
responsibility for injury, loss, or damage occasioned to any
person acting or refraining from action as a result of material
in this book whether or not such injury, loss, or damage in any
way is due to any negligent act or omission, breach of duty,
or default on the part of the publisher, the author, the editor,
or their respective employees or agents.

Publisher: Lucky Leslie Publishing

Cover Design: Lindi Craddock
Editor: Kirsten Rees | Book Editor & Author Coach
Foreword: Billy Schwer

Connect with the author Instagram: @simon_leslie21
www.luckyleslie.com

ACKNOWLEDGEMENTS

NATALIE, BENJY, ZAC, SCOTT, AND GEORGE. You are the reason I strive to get better every day.

To every current and past member of my teams, thank you for allowing me into your life and helping me on my journey. And for continuously pushing me to do more and get better.

Claudia Ace, you are the bravest girl ever - you inspired me to write this story.

Thank you, I appreciate you all.

WHITE BELT THINKING

CONTENTS

FOREWORD

THIS BOOK IS FILLED with so many powerful positive messages. It is a great read for anyone wanting to achieve greater things in their life.

As I read through the pages of this fable, it brought back many memories of my own personal journey. I had forty-five professional fights and fought three times for the world title before succeeding on my fourth attempt in 2001. This book is a hero's journey and I was honoured to be featured within these pages. While the story is one of a boxer, it's actually a story of hope, courage, and belief.

Many a day I was out of bed before the sun came up. I battled on through failure, disappointment, and heartbreak. The road to being a champion is a long one, a rollercoaster ride full of ups and downs. I think Simon has captured many of the emotions I faced in the boxing ring and also in the boxing ring of life since I've retired.

I hope you enjoy this book as much as I did.

Remember this, you do not have to be sick to get better.

Billy Schwer
Inspiring & Empowering people to live with Passion, Power & Purpose
www.billyschwer.com
@billyschwer

WHITE BELT THINKING

INTRODUCTION

THIS BOOK IS WRITTEN for the ambitious you. The you who had huge dreams, who wanted to achieve so much. The creative you and the brave you, the one that you see in the mirror every day.

As children, we dreamt so vividly and had lofty plans. Some of us found our purpose, some sold it for the security of a paycheck, healthcare, and a pension. But all of us have it in us. Sometimes, we need someone else to recognize it and help bring it to the fore. I have spent the last thirty years looking at ways to help people live their best lives, not be slaves to the system, and to enjoy going into their role every day.

Since March 2020, I have needed my mentors, coaches, and advisors to help me get through the toughest two years of my professional career, and solidify what it's all about and when enough is really enough. Through these conversations, I was reminded that I am world-class at spotting and developing talent and building meaningful relationships. I also learnt that it was a task that I continued to hone and improve month after month. The reason I stayed the course for so long is because I understood my role. I didn't worry about my weaknesses, I just kept improving what I was good at.

Thirty years of doing this provided evidence of a couple of things I am good at. With so many success stories along the way, I am proud to have been a mentor, coach, friend, father, and sounding board to many. That does not mean I didn't fail multiple times. I know I was harsh and also let down, disappointed, and failed some in this journey. In our little business, we had over a dozen marriages, babies, and relationships formed that will outlast me. I am proud of being a trusted advisor to many people, giving them belief, hope, and courage until they found their own. And boy, did some find their own.

The messages in this book have been honed over the last quarter-century, pasted on our walls and in our communication. The sheer fact you are reading this makes me happy.

We all have a gift inside of us. If the world hasn't seen yours yet, I hope this book encourages you to find it, or find someone to help you discover it.

This story is one of passion, focus, belief, language, overcoming challenges, clarity, gratitude, and finding the angels in your life. Remember, we know on what day we were born, we don't know how long we have on this planet. Make every day count and think like a beginner.

I would encourage you to do some of the exercises in this book to uncover who you are and who or what is holding you back.

A comprehensive workbook is available at *luckyleslie.com*

WHITE BELT THINKING

CHAPTER ONE

IS IT REALLY TRUE?

IT'S A FREEZING COLD November day in London. In one corner of the West Library, two friends are debating loudly. In a broad Irish accent, the young man Davie complains to the girl as he paces the floor.

"You know, it's easy for you Penny. You are like really privileged and your parents will always look out for you. Me, how can I ever succeed?" Davie gesticulates and shakes his head from side to side. "My father is a drunk, my mother works every hour God gives her, and I am here in London to escape the lack of opportunity in Ireland. There is nothing going for me right now."

Penny looks defeated as she leans forward on the desk.

"My accent holds me back, my results are poor, and frankly, I have no idea what I want to do with my life. You have the world at your feet. Me? I'm just a poor boy from a broken family with zero options. The recession in Ireland killed my family's business, they are barely living above the poverty line. I've come to the big smoke to help and I'm lost."

In the background is a graying, slightly overweight, older man reading the Financial Times. He speaks as he walks towards them. "Young man, is that really true?"

They both look up as he approaches them.

"Excuse me – I overheard you talking, actually everyone heard you complaining about your life, but is it really true?"

"Sadly, it is, why do you ask anyway?" says Davie.

"Young man, my name is Jonny Taffoir but my friends call me Taffy and I like to help people."

"Why?" asks Davie.

"Because I have always believed that the more people we help in life, the more life turns out the way you want for yourself. Listening to your story, it dawned on me that maybe you just need someone in your corner who believes in you."

"In my corner? Why did you mention corner?"

"It's just a metaphor, young man, someone to look out for you."

"You know, Mr Taffy—"

"Just Taffy," he replies.

"Taffy, when I was young, I dreamed that one day I could be a boxing champion, but life knocked that dream out of me. Now, life is just a bloody nightmare."

"It's important not to fold while life is unfolding, Davie. Will you do me a favor?"

"Sure."

"I want you to sit down there with a piece of blank paper. On one side, I want you to write down all the things that you want out of life, what you dreamt about as a child. On the other, I want you to write all the things that are stopping you right now from achieving those dreams. Mark that piece of paper with today's date 11/11," he says, tapping the date on the newspaper he was still holding, " and remember this moment as the moment you decided to change the odds in your favor. If you start with the end in mind and work backward, together we can make a plan to turn your setbacks into the biggest fightback your world has ever seen. Have you ever done anything like this before?"

"No, I haven't."

"Has anyone ever given you hope, belief, or courage? Write their names on the paper too, and on that other side write the people you think have held you back. I'm going to pop out and when I come back, we can review what you've done." He tucked his newspaper under his arm, turned about, and waddled off.

Davie turns to Penny and says, "What a fruit cake, let's get out of here."

"No Davie, do yourself a favor and listen to the old man. You spend so much time as a victim, he thinks he can help you. It's time for you to be a hero. Just spend ten minutes doing what he asked. You have nothing to lose, and I think you have a lot to gain."

WHEN TAFFY RETURNS, Davie is pages deep in his list. With a wry smile, he turned to Taffy.

"I'm kinda enjoying this. Still got a few things to add."

"Good," says Taffy. "When you are done, call me back over. This moment, young Davie, is about to be life-changing for you. Sometimes in life, all we need is for someone to believe in us. Just to be clear, a blank canvas allows us to think like a beginner. In most martial arts, you get a white belt as a new student. I tell everyone who will listen to adopt that thinking every single day. Think like a beginner and the world will present you with fresh opportunities daily."

CHAPTER TWO

THINKING LIKE A WHITE BELT

"WHO IS MR O'Rourke, Davie?" asks Taffy, reading the piece of paper Davie passed across the desk to him.

"He was my PE teacher," says Davie, "and he would always tell me I had wonderful energy, and that I was a natural athlete. He used to make me feel ten foot tall. And Mrs Finnegan, she was my English teacher. She told me I was the best storyteller in the world."

"So, as a boy, who was your hero?"

"I loved a boxer called Billy Schwer, he won the world title at the fourth attempt."

"And, as a boy, what did you want to be?"

"I really wanted to be a boxer. But because we were so poor, I had to do two jobs and had no time to train. I came to London to make a difference for my family."

"Who or what held you back?"

"My dad really brought me down. He used to tell me I was useless and would never amount to much, that I was a drain on the family. My sister Margie got married early and escaped, leaving me to watch my ma and pa fight and bicker." Davie pauses, looking at the piece of paper on the desk between the two of them and then back up at Taffy and Penny. "I just realized how lucky I am to be here and not still acting as referee to those two. You know what, Taffy, this has been a really useful exercise. I really have got some talents; I really did have dreams and ambitions. I just let life get in the way."

"That's right dear Davie, you clearly are a natural orator, and instead of using it as a force for good, you have been using it to tear yourself down. You wrote 'find love, passion, and money' atop the page, it's a great start. You might not be who you want to be, but at least you are not who you used to be. It's not too late to live out your dreams. My advice to you, young man, is study these notes," he says, tapping the page, "work out where your passion is and drive a freight train towards your goals.

Mark my words Davie, language is key to success. Use your words wisely, you must have the right mindset during difficult times. There is no time for drama in these dramatic times, Davie. This could be the moment you look back on in many years and think 'this conversation changed the direction of my life'. One conversation can change the world, that's why I talk to everybody and ignore nobody.

Be kind to people dispensing advice to you Davie," he says, smiling over at Penny, "and make your own mind up. There is only one person in the world who can help you or destroy you, and that's the person in the mirror."

He stands up and then pushes the piece of paper back towards Davie. "I have written my telephone number on your paper in case you ever need to ask me anything. By the way, I always wanted to go to the Pyramids and to live near the sea, you just need to work out how we make those dreams come true. Good luck and remember this, your dreams are talking to you every day; starve the negative noise and listen to them."

WHITE BELT THINKING

CHAPTER THREE

SUCCESS IS DRIVEN BY
HOW BIG YOUR BELIEF IS

OVER THE NEXT couple of months, Davie realized Taffy was right; he did have the gift of the gab. After going after various roles, he finally settled on selling pharmaceuticals as he really loved selling and engaging with customers. At the same time, he decided to pursue his passion for acting. The night classes also helped with his ability to speak more clearly and communicate better with customers and colleagues.

The knowledge of medicine and selling are a wonderful combination, he would tell anyone who would listen. Davie realized he actually loved learning. He remembered Mrs Finnegan telling him, "You should always be a lifelong learner!"

It was all starting to make sense now. Life was on the up, he even met someone special - Alyson, although everyone called her Aly. Six weeks in, he and Aly were really becoming fond of each other and so, he asked her to be his girlfriend. Davie enjoys her company, her drive and zest for life. She would lift his spirits when he was down and make him smile when he was sad, he hoped he was doing the same for her. She was a young woman from Atlanta, who was studying medicine in London. Long, flowing blonde hair, a real Georgia peach. Life felt amazing and things were finally starting to look up for the first time in his life.

On the fifteenth of July, as Davie wanders around his local area, he stumbles across a boxing gym. The smell of sweat, leather gloves, and boxing bags waft out as he paused at the door.

Strangely, it was raining, it never normally rained on St Swithin's Day. Apparently, it was on this day that the great flood started for Noah, and if it rained on St Swithin's it would rain for forty days. Amazing what facts you remember from school. As the rain begins to soak through his clothes and drip down his neck, he ducks through the door to get inside.

A chubby, short man welcomes him in. "How can I help ya, sunshine?"

"I once had a dream that I could be a world champion."

"Yeah son, I had a dream that I would be James Bond!"

"No, I am serious. As a kid I had speedy hands and quick feet, I was agile and no one could hit me."

"Why don't you come in tomorrow and show us what you got?"

Davie nodded enthusiastically and left, feeling excited about the chance to test out his childhood dream again.

THE NEXT MORNING at 6am, Davie arrived ready for his workout; he strips down to his shorts and vest, put on the wraps and started warming up. Skipping and bag-work followed press ups, sit ups, burpees, crunches galore – the pain was excruciating, he wanted to throw up. It was horrible, but at the same time something very special sparked inside him; the love was back. His passion had been rekindled.

"Not as fit as you thought you were," says the trainer. "You have got some moves though, my boy."

Davie heard Taffy's words reverberate in his head, don't be dramatic amongst the drama. After ninety minutes of rigorous training, he got changed to leave.

The old man chuckled as Davie says, "I'll be back tomorrow."

"We'll see," he says. "Hope the pain is not too much for you."

Davie left exhausted, but the fire in his belly was back. His life had already turned around so much in just nine months, and now he had found something he was truly excited about. As Davie skips down the road, he thinks of Mr O'Rourke – "One day, Davie, you could really go far in this world."

Those words gave him the belief he needed. "Success is driven by belief" was graffitied on the wall near his home, and how true that was; for the first time in his life he had a cause to believe in. Davie thinks to himself, some say success is impossible, others say it's inevitable. It's time to decide which camp I wanna be in.

For the next two weeks, Davie was at the gym every morning at 6am. Stan, the gym manager, was impressed with his fitness and agility. Was this a hobby or something bigger?, he wondered.

For the very first time in his life, Davie loved everything he did, he was happy. Whatever he did, he outworked everyone, he was first in and last out. He had a job he loved, a girl he cared for, and he was auditioning for walk-on acting roles. He spoke to his parents every week, even his newfound energy rubbed off on them.

Were they proud of me? he wondered. His problem was he loved them all. As he thought back to that letter in the library, the words, LOVE, MONEY, PASSION that he had written on the piece of paper were here. Maybe Taffy was right about committing your vision to paper. Was it time to pick up the phone and ask him for some more direction?

Davie thinks to himself, is it unrealistic for things to change so quickly? No, your situation can change in a heartbeat, as long as you have a clear idea of what you want, and are prepared to work harder than your old self to make it happen. I found a cause to believe in. And I trusted myself.

WHITE BELT THINKING

CHAPTER FOUR

WTF

"A FUNNY THING happened at work today, Aly. A flyer went round about a white-collar boxing event in October and I've decided to enter myself to fight."

A brief silence follows. "Davie," she says, in her deep southern drawl, "You and I are in a great place, work is great, and you are working so hard on all of your dreams, why put yourself in danger by fighting? I have heard so many horror stories about people getting hurt doing these amateur fights."

Wow, he thinks to himself. How can she not support my dream? Did I not share enough how much boxing means to me? Maybe I should have explained it differently. With boxing everyone has a plan until they get hit. That was my first setback this year, how am I going to come back from this? She's right though, I am in a great place; she loves me, work loves me, and I feel amazing in all aspects of my life. Why should I give all that up on a boyhood dream?

He moves closer, pulling her into a hug and she wraps her arms around him too.

But life is full of disappointments, and when things are not going the best way, why do we throw in the towel so easily? Now is the time, I need to talk to Taffy.

"Aly, I am going for a walk, I just need to clear my head okay."

The phone rings for what seems like an age, the voices in his head are arguing, only silenced when the quiet voice says hello.

"I hope I'm not disturbing you, sir, my name is Davie Murphy. We met at the library last year."

"I remember you, Davie, you were down on your luck. You sound very different, young man, your voice is filled with positive energy and confidence. What has happened to you?"

Davie shares his story of how things were on the up. All his good fortune from the past nine months. He finally got around to his dilemma.

"You see Taffy, life is wonderful, I am so happy, but I —"

Taffy interrupts. "We don't say BUT, we say AND."

"Life is wonderful, I am so happy AND I want to have a go at fighting."

"So, you want to have your cake and eat it too?" Taffy replies.

"I guess so."

"Okay, in circumstances like this we need to get you focused. Let's look at the problem – you are busy being busy, you have many projects and something you need to decide is WTF."

"WTF, as in what the f***?"

"No, dear boy, I think swearing is for those who lack linguistic skills. WTF – where to focus. It's white paper time again, Davie. Why do you want to box? Who are you doing it for? What's the upside and what's the worst that can happen and can you live with that? This is a time for your character to come through and shine. In order to do boxing, what do you need to sacrifice, who do you need to sacrifice and how will you feel if you do not follow your dream?"

Ten minutes later, the phone went down and Davie began to think and write.

WHITE BELT THINKING

.

CHAPTER FIVE

LOOKING FOR THE SIGNS

THAT EVENING THINGS were a bit frosty between Aly and Davie. They made small talk over dinner then he decided to sit down and reconcile his thoughts.

How could this one man, who I met by accident, have such wisdom and such a profound effect on my life? Why is it the people who have the most impact in your life are the ones who you meet by accident and have no agenda? You need people who will add value to your life, not hold you back.

Davie decided to sleep on it and see how he felt in the morning. After tossing and turning all night, he arrived at the gym at 6am. Stan noticed a difference in his energy.

"What's up, champ?" he asked. "You don't seem your usual top-of-the-morning self."

"Stan, I want to take part in a white-collar boxing event and Aly is not happy for me."

"Son, it's now time to see if your boyhood dreams are able to come true and to decide if you want regret or not in your life. We mostly regret the things we don't do. You've got talent but you don't need to do this. You could just keep it as a hobby, use it to stay fit, but not build your life around boxing."

He walks over to stand right in front of Davie and looks him in the eyes.

"Life will always ask us questions. Most of us have the answers but are too scared to respond. We always know the answers, and it's only us who can decide. You have to decide if you want to be an amateur or a professional. Both choices are fine. There is a saying that in the spring, when it's cold, you have to decide if you want to commit to the journey, if you really want to do it. Because winter will always ask you what you did all spring and summer."

Davie finishes his workout on his route home, thinking through the pros and cons of what he wanted. He certainly didn't want to miss an opportunity to see if he could be someone in the world of boxing, but he also didn't want to mess up the good life he had started to create. Deep in his thoughts and not looking where he is going, he bumps into an elderly lady.

"I'm so sorry, madam."

She turns to him and says, "Whatever it is that is concerning you, think about this, young man, you have to believe something wonderful is about to happen." With that, she was on her way.

It's a sign from someone, Davie thinks to himself, I've got this white belt mentality Taffy told me about now, so what should I do in this instance? He pauses in his walk and straightens up. I am going to make something wonderful happen. I am going to get Aly on my side, and I am going to focus and commit. This is my dream, and no one is going to stop me living it.

WHITE BELT THINKING

CHAPTER SIX

MAN PLANS AND GOD LAUGHS

"ALY, I LOVE YOU more than I have loved anyone in my life."

"Aw that's sweet, Davie," Aly replies.

"But - I mean and - I want you to support me in my dream. I want to see if I can be a professional boxer. It's what I wanted all my life, and I have to at least give it a shot. I don't want to lose you, but I don't want to regret not chasing my dream either. I have to prove to my father that I am capable of being somebody."

"Davie, we have to put a wedge in between your stories. Let's not live in the past or the future, that's living nowhere. We have to be present, and I like the phrase until now; until now people thought you might not amount to much, but right now in this moment you have to believe everybody – including your father – is behind you, supporting you. You have to do this for the right reasons, not to prove anything to anyone. This has to be your dream, because you are good enough, and if you are not good enough, that's okay too."

She sat down and gestured for him to do the same. Davie sat in the seat next to her and reached over to take her hand.

"You are a brilliant boyfriend," she says, "a brilliant salesman and storyteller. From now onwards, we have to live in the present and focus on what we both can control. My father once told me motivation is like a warm bath, it's lovely for fifteen minutes then it wears off. If you are going to do this properly, we both need to make sure we have a plan for success. You have to drop things that are not important. I read once, 'when you stop making excuses, you will start to discover your results'. Life is a series of magic moments, Davie, we are going to create many of these together, and we are going to have challenges along the way."

And at that very moment the phone rang, an anxious voice at the other end of the line. "Davie, your dad's died, please come home."

Davie began to cry. Why, why at the very moment I made a decision to show him, did he have to go? He packed his bags quickly while Aly helped him make arrangements to head back Ireland.

CHAPTER SEVEN
NO MORE EXCUSES

THE FLIGHT HOME was bumpy, and as the plane landed at Dublin Airport, his sister Margie was there to greet him. A ninety-minute drive between green fields and through rain brought him to the house. His mum was looking really old and frail, the last couple of years had been tough on her.

"Hi Ma," Davie says as he hugs and holds on to her tightly.

"Oh I have missed you, son."

"Aly sends her love too, she's sorry she couldn't get time off work at such short notice."

"She's a good one that Aly, you send her our love when you speak to her."

Over the next few days, mother and son catch up and she explains how his father had drunk so much over the years that his body just couldn't support him any longer. But at least, he had died peacefully in his sleep. She was still working two jobs and financially they were a mess.

"Mum, I didn't know it had got this bad. I want

to help you. Over the next six months, I will send you enough money so you can quit one job and, by the end of the year, I want to set you up so you can enjoy life."

Tears rolled down her face as they hugged each other. "I so wanted to prove Dad wrong, Mum, I wanted to show him that I could become someone. I'm going to become a champion, Mum, mark my words, I will make you proud."

"Darling, we were already so proud of you, all the messages and letters you sent us made us happy. Your dad was so proud of you in his own way. You wait till the funeral – all his friends heard him wax lyrical about his son doing so well in London."

"I had no idea, Mum."

"Your dad loved you, Davie. Whatever you do in life, you must know that you are loved. You know, as a family, we were hard workers and although our business was ruined by the recession we never gave up. And I know you, son, you will outwork everyone. It's in your genes. It's time for you to show the world what you've got. My father used to say to us, the only satisfactory aim in life is to achieve an unattainable goal, that's what we want for you."

AFTER THE FUNERAL, his dad's friends shared stories and unveiled stuff Davie had never known about his father. On the way through town Davie sees Mr O'Rourke, now looking so old. He stops to say hello and tell him what he was about to do.

"Listen, my son, you do this for your parents, for our village, and for Ireland."

Davie leaves Ireland with wonderful memories and stories, his head held high. It was now time to show the world what he had. He remembered what Aly said before he left, 'when you stop making excuses, you start to see the results'. From this day forward he promised himself, no more excuses.

WHITE BELT THINKING

CHAPTER EIGHT

BEHAVE LIKE THE PERSON YOU WANT TO BE

THE NEXT MORNING, Davie is at the gym before anyone else arrives. When the coach turns up, he greets Davie with a hug and is genuinely sorry for his loss.

"Coach, this is the new me," he says. "No excuses, I am going to be the hardest worker in this gym, I will outwork everyone. Set me the most ridiculous targets and I will beat them; set a diet and I will stick to it. I want to be a champion. I am no longer doing this as an amateur, from this day forward I will be a professional. Winter is going to ask me what I did all summer, and I want to have all the answers. So, let's map out the journey from the belt backwards. Know this, Coach, every day I will have a white belt mentality."

"What's that, Davie?"

"It's the beginner's mentality, seeing everything with a fresh set of eyes, not clouded by what I think I know. It's being open to new ideas, and asking myself constantly, 'What did I do wrong there? Where and how can I do better next time? What do I need to focus on for the next day and get really good at? What did I learn from this? What did I do to make this happen?' When you have a white belt mentality, you see the world differently. Everything is an opportunity to improve. The best bit – there is no finish line, every day is day one. Jeff Bezos of Amazon always refers to his day one letters. I wrote my letter in a library in London and that's my day one." He unfolded the piece of paper he had carried in his wallet every day.

Coach pointed to the date written at the top. "You know what 11:11 is, Davie?"

"No, I don't."

"It's the sign of the angel, somebody is watching over you. You had help from an angel to get you here. Keep an eye out for those four numbers."

Davie nods. "We need to create a route map to follow, I want to have a plan to stick to, and let's start with the end in mind. We need to amass a team that can make this work, Coach – I want to find the best mentors, coaches, trainers, physios so that all the advice I get is world class. So long as my bills are paid and my mum is taken care of, I want to throw every spare penny I've saved over the past year at this, and boy I made some great commission check. Even if I am an amateur right now, I want to think, train, believe, and behave like I am a champion already. I want a champion's mindset."

"Sounds like a plan, Davie, it's good to forecast a positive future, it's important not to let your past hold you back. But right now, I need you where your feet are – get down and start your push ups. Stay present, stay in the now."

Davie raised a wry smile. "You got it, Coach, and from this day forward I'm going for the 'one more' method."

"And what's that one, Davie?"

"Whatever you or anyone else asks me to do, I will do one more. One more push up, one more call, and one more email. I am going to be the hardest worker in the room."

WHITE BELT THINKING

CHAPTER NINE
THINKING TIME

THE NIGHT OF the white-collar boxing was closing in fast, and the training had been intense. Davie had trained the program of a champion, not an amateur contest for working people. He was feeling strong in body and mind. Aly was coming round to the idea and being more supportive.

"Today I am going to spend time with you," he says to her. "We are going to just be present, no talk about boxing or work, just us. I know it's really important in our busy schedules to find time for us. How about we go for a walk in Richmond, by the river? "

Aly nods and grabs her coat and they head out together.

As they walk along the riverside, Davie thinks to himself, even amongst the madness I needed to find 'thinking time'. Time to reflect on how far he has come since that chance meeting in the library. One thing Taffy had said was, "Always remember where you started, it helps keep the journey real." Too many people get caught up in the doing, rather than just being. We are human beings, not human doings. Being with oneself, being at peace, being a good partner, being someone others can rely on and, most importantly, being honest to yourself.

"I love to be by the water and reflect. It's been a turbulent few months, and I realize you and I have not spent much quality time together."

Aly squeezed his hand and smiled. The day was superb, they had coffee and walked, talked, and listened to songs that made them feel alive and in love.

Over lunch, looking out over the River Thames, Aly says, "This is what we needed, it's what I needed from you. I know how much you appreciate me. I know you love me, yet at times, I play second fiddle to your ambitions. So, you taking the time to show me how much you care and just to listen to me means so much. Let's make sure we do this more often."

"Aly, it's our life and from this day on, we are going to find time to do the things that we want to do as well as everything else I promise. There is no reason why we can't enjoy our lives and work hard, train hard, and achieve our dreams. We've only got one shot at this so let's make it a good one. No more excuses."

As they get back to the car, they notice the road that they are parked in is Love Lane. The stars were aligning.

ALWAYS LOOK FOR the signs. They are everywhere.

WHITE BELT THINKING

CHAPTER TEN

IT'S GAME TIME

THE FIGHT NIGHT arrived, and butterflies were circling in Davie's stomach.

"Coach, I've never felt like this before."

"Davie, welcome to the world of high performance. It's a good thing, it's all about the language you use. Are you nervous or are you excited, which gives you more energy? Excitement, right?"

"You're right, just that simple reframing makes me feel better already."

"Well, the emotions are the same, raised heartbeat, sweaty palms and brain going a hundred miles an hour. The word 'excitement' is positive and forward-looking with encouragement, versus 'nervous', which is predicting a negative future. It's all about having faith not fear, Davie. Your opponent won't know what hit him when you get into the ring. Remember, you are only a white belt and see things in that perspective. Channel the energy through your body. Don't punch with your hands, punch with your body, with your positive, believing energy."

AND AT THE END of the first round, Davie danced back to the corner.

"That was exhilarating, Coach, it felt incredible."

"Your combinations were like a seasoned champion, Davie. He didn't know where the next punch was coming from, you can tell you are really enjoying this experience."

Davie looks up at the crowd and spots a familiar face, his friend Penny who he hadn't seen in a long while. She waves at him and he grins back. His eyes drift until he sees Aly out the corner of his eye, she blows him a kiss. A warm feeling deep inside was alive. The fight continues and round after round. Davie punches and moves, toying with his opponent. He wanted the experience, he wanted to get rounds under his belt. The bell went for the final round.

"Knock him out now, Davie, he's getting lazy, you have done the hard work."

At 1 minute, 11 seconds into the round, his opponent hit the canvas. The referee jumps in, and the fight was over. The journey had begun, yes, this was just an amateur boxing night, but what Davie displayed was determination, courage, patience, and class.

"These are the qualities of a champion," says Coach, "and remember, if we train hard, we win easy."

Penny came through the crowd and smiles widely at him. She looks tired, older than he remembers her even though it was only a year since he had seen her last.

"Congratulations Davie, you will brilliant."

"Penny, it's so good to see you. How are you?"

"Not so good Davie. Times have been tougher than expected, even with all my 'privilege' as you called it. But seeing you tonight has been inspiring! I think I'm going to do what Taffy requested of you and write it all down. See if I can turn it all around like you have."

He smiles at her and then she disappears into the crowd just as quickly as she appeared. He is surrounded by people shaking his hand and wanting his attention. Also in the audience that night were a few ex-boxers; the story was about to get interesting.

WHITE BELT THINKING

CHAPTER ELEVEN

DO WHAT YOU SAY YOU WILL DO

"THAT WAS MIGHTY impressive, young man," says an older guy as he walks up to Davie. "Is this just for fun or are you thinking about taking this a little more seriously?"

"Serious, sir, I am going to be a champion."

"One step at a time, my young friend. You have incredible movement and agility, you have a good brain, but you need better people to help you if you want to be the best. I have had the pleasure of training two world champions; would you like to come to my gym and show us what you got?"

"Sure, what have I got to lose? Coach, are you okay with that?"

"Davie, as you get better you need to surround yourself with better people, better thinkers, and find the best trainers. You need to work on your mindset, you need to spar with better boxers who will find your weaknesses. This is a wonderful moment, don't forget this as the journey progresses, it's another marker on the road to your destination."

"I'll see you tomorrow sir, what time does your gym open? I like to be the first one in."

"I love that attitude, see you at 5am tomorrow."

Davie gulped. I just finished my first fight, and I am committing to being up at 4am to be there for 5am. I am not going to be an amateur anymore, I am on the road to winning and it starts in his gym at 5am.

THE NEXT MORNING, he wakes up feeling a little stiff, but he leaps out of bed and heads for the gym. When he gets there at 4:55, the timings on the door say it opens at 6am. He was about to get angry and disappointed when he spots the chap from last night in the reflection of the gym windows.

"What's up, champ?"

"I thought you were testing me, getting me here this early when the gym doesn't open for an hour."

"Davie, I was testing you. I wanted to see how much you want this opportunity. I have to say it was difficult getting out of bed this early even without fighting last night, so I am super impressed by you."

"Coach, there is no time for celebration. Michael Jordan was back in the gym after he won his sixth ring. This is time for making magic happen and delivering on the promises I made to my mum."

"I think you and I are going to have some fun."

"Coach, what do I call you?"

"My name is Erroll, but Coach is just fine."

Davie in life, it's always about finding the best people you can, and learning from them. The Japanese call it Kaizen, its constant and never ending improvement.

WHITE BELT THINKING

CHAPTER TWELVE

PLANNING TIME IS IMPORTANT

OVER THE NEXT couple of weeks, training got tougher, the recovery was harder, and combining it with work and keeping his relationship with Aly good was challenging. It felt like he was setting himself on fire to keep everyone else warm. Something had to give. It was the first time in a long while he felt a little broken.

His first professional fight was less than a month away, and he needed to find a way to keep everything in check. He also needed a day away to be together with Aly, so he organized a day at the races. They arrived at the racecourse to a beautiful table overlooking the course, champagne for Aly and water for him, a day of 'us time' was needed. They spent time planning the places they wanted to visit and created their own 'hundred list', a list of a hundred things they wanted and needed to do in the next couple of years.

"It's so important to plan our adventure together; the last couple of months we've both been so busy and let things slip again. Our relationship is the most important thing to me, Aly, even if at times we don't feel it."

"Davie, I understand," she says and reaches across the table to take his hand. "Now, the horse in the next race is called 'Becoming a Champion', so let's put a few pounds on it."

When the horse won by three lengths at 8/1 Davie and Aly hug and cheer. It was a sign, he thinks, this is my time, I am on the journey to greatness. I am happy, I have everything a man could ask for. A happy life.

In that moment, he felt he needed to do something spontaneous. Davie drops to one knee in front of Aly. With the can ring off a coke can, he proposes to Aly. It wasn't going to fit but it was the question that mattered – and her answer. After a long pause and with tears in her eyes, she says, "Yes".

Davie could not believe how much his life had turned around. Tomorrow, I will ring Taffy and share the great news.

CHAPTER THIRTEEN

DON'T BE UNKIND TO YOURSELF

THE PHONE SEEMED to ring for ages before the old man picked up.

"Mornin' Taffy, it's Davie Murphy. How are you?"

"My dear boy, I'm well as can be, how about your good self?"

"I have much to share with you. Sadly, my father passed away, I had my first fight, I found a new trainer, and I proposed to Aly," he blurted out, before drawing breath.

"Wow, haven't you been busy! I am sad to hear the news of your father. Did you see him before he passed?"

"I didn't, but my mum and his friends shared so many stories about how proud of me he was, I never knew. And you know that I had beaten myself up with so many stories until that point."

"You know Davie, a funny thing about us humans is we are quite unkind to ourselves; we tell ourselves stories about how bad we are, how our bodies are no good, how we are not clever enough, and on and on and on. We can be really mean to ourselves but if there is one lesson in this, it is that we have to be kind and considerate to ourselves. You see, the brain doesn't know if you are telling the truth or lying to yourself. Your words are gold, and if you don't use them kindly, they end up destroying you. When I met you, you were broken, spouting complaints to anyone who would listen to you."

"Yeah, I still remember that day in the library when I was gnawing poor Penny's ear off about how bad I thought my life was, as if it's someone else's responsibility to fix things."

"Now look at you, you are about to become a champion, a successful salesman, a husband, and an all-round good human. It's all about energy Davie, let's meet and talk about the importance of energy. I would like to come to see you train at the gym. I'll see if I can help bring some others that can help you progress your skills. I am so pleased for you and cannot wait to catch up."

"I'd love if you come see me train. And it all started because of you. Thanks Taffy."

At that point, the phone went dead. He's right; I was unnecessarily mean to myself for way too long. Once I changed the narrative, once I started believing in myself, my whole world began to change. I am excited to learn about energy. I've always had lots of energy, so it will be good to understand what it's all about.

Davie thinks to himself, if our friends talked to us, how we talk to ourselves, we would not be friends for very long. It had to stop, I am a hero not a victim.

WHITE BELT THINKING

CHAPTER FOURTEEN

KEEP MOVING FORWARD

THE GYM SMELT of sweat and testosterone-filled men. Taffy saw Davie in the ring, going through a proper session. With each round, a new opponent and throwing different combinations. It looked tough and grueling. He sat himself down and watched patiently as the session progressed. Erroll came over to say hello.

"Hi, I'm Erroll," says his old coach, with a slightly territorial-hippo welcome. He held a 'you are in my place of worship' aura.

"Hello there, my name is Jonny Taffoir, but my friends call me Taffy. You know, I met this young boy a year or so back and have been helping him find his why, his purpose and reason for being. He tells me you are a championship trainer; how do you feel about his prospects for success?"

"It's still early days, but he is showing promise. He's definitely talented, he has the drive and determination, we just got to see if he can do it on the big stage—"

Taffy butted in. "I do love the Michael Tyson quote, *'everyone has a plan until you get hit'*, or something like that."

"Yes, I like that too, we have to see how the first big fight pans out and then we can move forward."

Taffy interjected again. "I would love to be part of your team, I can really help with bringing mindset, movement, and wellbeing coaches to the team. Would you be open to that, Erroll?"

"I have a lot of these," replies Errol, "but I would welcome hearing and meeting your people too, and whoever is the best we can work with. After all, we want to see Davie achieve his dream." His tone became more friendly and warm.

"It's a long road from here," says Taffy, "and we can only do our best, Erroll. Our best today has to be marginally better than yesterday's best. That's progress. Some progress is micro and some is huge. We all, as humans, want to keep moving forward."

"I love KMF, it stands for keep moving forward," Erroll responds, "you will see it in huge letters in my office. As long as there is tiny progress every day, I believe we are on the way to a better place. I am a huge believer in faith over fear, Taffy. I believe we all need faith in our lives. If we have a cause to believe in that is bigger than us, life is easier to live."

"I do love that phrase. Although I always say never want things to always be easier, just teach me how to deal with whatever life throws at me."

"That's so true, I believe God won't give me anything that I can't handle, Taffy. I just wish he didn't trust me so much."

The two old guys were chuckling to themselves as Davie walks over. "You two seem to be getting on well," he says.

"Your friend here, Davie, is a very wise man. It's good to have two brains instead of one to help you achieve your dream," says Erroll.

"Erroll, it was a pleasure to meet you and I am very much looking forward to the future. I'm going to explain energy to Davie over lunch," says Taffy. He turns to Davie. "Go grab a quick shower, and we can head out. "

WHITE BELT THINKING

CHAPTER FIFTEEN

ENERGY IS EVERYTHING AND EVERYTHING IS ENERGY

SAT IN THE OLD, quaint pub opposite the gym, Taffy began. "Everything is energy, Davie, that drink and even this food. You see, what energy you put into your body is what drives you forward. Energy is vital for our success; you hear people described as the life and soul of the party? That's saying their energy is strong, and engaging, and welcoming. Hugs, kisses, and love are high vibrational energy, as are powerful stories, affirmations, and kindness. Saying thank you and having appreciation also shows beautiful energy."

"So what's negative energy?"

"When we are overtired, eating the wrong foods, complaining, talking badly or negatively about people, being rude, not laughing or smiling at people. These all convey negative energy. With just one smile, you can change someone's demeanor. Think about a situation where you felt nervous, scared, or worried and with one smile the whole situation changed. Our thoughts become real things, so it's so important to think good ones. When we are clear where we are going, when we have a concrete plan, when we are positive and kind, our energy levels rise."

"What happens then?"

"We find more energy, we attract more like-minded people into our life – just look at who and what you have attracted recently, it's amazing. You went about life with the right intentions and attracted like-minded people, you also removed people who were 'draining' your energy. I always say the process of getting what you want is writing it down. That creates a kind of energy in your brain which drives you to figure out how it can come true. Our brain has this magical way of making the right things (and sometimes the wrong things) happen. We need good sleep, it's so important that we sleep well, eat well, read, and consume positive information. It's good to share your energy with others and be the beacon they are looking for. Don't be a door-to-door salesman with your advice."

"What do you mean?"

"Be a good listener, only dispense your opinion if it's asked for. Don't go around telling people what you know, stop being that know-it-all person, even if you are right and do it from a place of kindness, it's never received that way. If people ask, then you may offer your opinion or thinking, that way you will always be valued as a source of inspiration. When your energy is high, you attract so much goodness, and you bounce around like the Duracell bunny. Be aware though, when you use your energy up, you need to know when to relax, recharge, and rest. Even supercars need servicing and maintenance. Energy is one of the most wonderful things we all have, just some of us don't know how to use it for good."

Davie finishes chewing his food and takes a sip of water. "In what way?"

"How many people do you see complaining about all the negative news or putting energy drinks, drugs, alcohol, and too much coffee into their bodies every day? They need their fix of something to get them through. On the other hand, when you are in balance, when you sleep well, have good quality foods and consume positive content, spend time with like-minded people, you are a Ferrari of a human being. You know everyone wants to drive a Ferrari. Yet it still needs servicing, it still needs fuel, it still needs looking after. I cannot tell you how important energy is to be a happy, kind, and successful human."

"What about money, Taffy?"

"Money has low vibrational energy. You see, if you do the right things, you will attract more money; if you do good quality work, you'll get promoted and that will bring more money. If you have more energy than anyone else, you can work harder and smarter, think clearer, that will lead to more money. I also see it when people are scared or have a scarcity mindset and they get money, it gives them the wrong energy, they waste it, they lose it, they spend it unwisely. My belief is there is always more money, just be in the right energy mindset and you will attract it. The same will go with the people you attract, be careful when you make money where your focus goes. As you start to perform, new people will be attracted by your power and energy and you need to be careful who you let in. Money can cause the wrong behaviors, both to make it and to keep it. There is always more of everything you desire, apart from one thing Davie."

"What's that?"

"Time. There are always opportunities to make more money, the same can't be said for time. On that note, I have to run; your training today was mighty impressive. Keep going and I'll check in from time to time and bring you some interesting people to help you on your journey to the top. I do not have one doubt that you can do this. See you soon Davie."

CHAPTER SIXTEEN
TIME FOR EQUANIMITY

THERE IS A WEEK to go to until his first fight weigh in, he is a few pounds over where he needs to be. Davie was about to think some negative thoughts when the energy conversation replayed in his head.

I can do this, I know what I need to control, I know what I need to do. In seconds, the worry passed right through him. How easy was that.

Aly interrupted his thoughts. "How are you feeling, Davie?"

"I'm feeling confident. I think I'm ready. The next week is about me finding time to feel good. Training is much lighter this week and I am going to consume as much positive stuff as I can to get my mind in a good place. Taffy sent me some podcasts to listen to and some videos to watch from some really interesting people. I am really finding my zone, Aly.

"Let's walk plenty this week, let's spend some time together in nature. It's important for you to be grounded, Davie, I know it sounds a little tree-huggy, but getting out in nature is so good for your preparation."

"I believe you," says Davie. When she smiles and walks off, he plugs in his headphones and listens to a podcast on living in high-performance.

The next morning, after a light workout, Aly and Davie drive out to the country and set off on a nice long walk.

"You know, Aly, this podcast I listened to yesterday talked about breathing, diet, sleep, nature, and thinking time as some of the most important aspects of living in the performance zone. Much of this stuff I had heard from my coaches, but actually doing it with you is special."

As they walk, they both take a series of deep breaths, in and then breathing out.

"I feel my head clearing, Aly. Let's keep it going."

They spot a bench by a pond, and for the next hour sit watching the ducks and swans gracefully floating around the pond.

"Look at that swan," says Aly, "on the surface he looks calm and relaxed, but I'll bet under the water he is kicking like crazy. That's us as humans, we all try to be calm, but our brains and organs are working really hard and testing us all the time, with thoughts, emotions and challenges. Davie, the breathing gives you time to respond, slows the world down for a minute; it allows us to respond without reacting. These are all going to be powerful when you fight. Think of the swan, stay calm despite everything, breathe and keep your composure, and if you can do that you will find yourself two or even three steps ahead of your opponent. Have you ever heard of equanimity, Davie?"

"No, what's that?"

"It's being able to stay calm under pressure. You know, when all around you are losing theirs, it's your job to stay in the game. That's one of the true qualities you have developed this year. When we first met, you had a real short fuse, but now, you are composed, and I think it's the most beautiful quality in you. No one or no thing gets to you anymore. You are becoming the most balanced person I have ever met."

"What a kind thing to say Aly, and something I am going to cherish. I feel balanced, it's exactly the quality I want to have and display. Come on, let's walk back to the car. This has been a beautiful day. I keep saying it, but finding time to do different things is so important for our wellbeing. Tomorrow, I want to spend time in the pool. Coach thinks it will help with my breathing and stretching."

WHITE BELT THINKING

CHAPTER SEVENTEEN

FOCUS WHERE YOUR FEET ARE

THE WEIGH-IN went to plan. In a few hours the fight would be behind him, just two more fights ahead. Davie is sat in the changing room, breathing and calming himself down. Asking himself great questions. How will I react if I get hit? What will I do if I am struggling. How will I celebrate?

Taffy walks into the changing room. "How are you Davie? Ready to win your first big fight?"

"You know Taffy I wish my dad was here tonight to see this, he would have been so proud. I just hope I am good enough."

"Well let me tell you a few things Davie, if you live in your past or current way of thinking, there is no room to grow into your new improved lifestyle."

"What do you mean?"

"We have moved on from doing things for your father, that is an old story. Being self-deprecating and humble, that's a current story. If you want to stay in the past or live in the current place you are, keep telling yourself this old dialogue."

"How would you reframe it, Taffy? I cannot wait to win the fight and move forward to even better opponents. To create a legacy for my family, for me to show my children and tell them how much I love them while I am still alive. To be an even better version of me every single day."

"You see, in life Davie, too many people are letting their past hold them back, and letting their future be too scary to move forward. So, they live in a place of never having enough, being jealous of others, and not appreciating anything." As Taffy finishes, the bell rings. The fight was about to be called.

"Sounds like a sign to me, Davie." Taffy smiles. "Be present, be optimistic and start living the new life, the new way of seeing the world. By the way, you have a guest watching you tonight, your hero Billy Schwer is in the audience. I asked him to come and see you. So, make sure you impress him."

CHAPTER EIGHTEEN

TIME TO SHINE

"WELL, SUNSHINE, THAT was mighty impressive: a knockout in the third," says Billy as he walks into the changing room. "How did that feel?"

"Oh my goodness, I am so glad to meet you, I watched all of your fights," says Davie.

"Our friend Taffy told me your story. You seemed to have so much time and composure tonight. What's your secret?

"It's equanimity, Mr Schwer."

"Sounds complicated to me. Equa-nim-ity. What does that mean?"

"It's about staying calm under pressure. My girlfriend, I mean fiancé, told me that's what I do."

"Well I don't care what you call it, it gives you time to get your punches away. Keep training hard, Davie, you could have a career ahead of you in this game. They won't be all as easy as you made it tonight. Enjoy the win and I will keep an eye out for you."

"Thank you so much, Mr Schwer."

"Just call me Billy."

"Thank you for coming, Billy," he says, as Aly runs over and hugs him.

"My hero," she squeals, "you were like the swan, calm and composed, and legs did all the work."

Davie sits down in the corner and breathes deeply. He thinks to himself, how do I frame this in a way that creates my positive future self. That was a good performance, I outboxed my opponent. I have lots of growth to come, yet I am really happy with the steps I took today to make tomorrow even better. He chuckles to himself. I'm even thinking in positive futuring. Futuring is the art of creating the future you want to live in. So this my dream with a plan.

"Davie, tonight can we celebrate?" Aly asks.

"Coach, what do you think?" He turns to Erroll.

"Davie, have the next three days off. Spend them together, enjoy all the things that you have been missing, and I'll see you back in the gym on Monday to plan out the next phase of the journey. You were great tonight, and I love the equa-thingy too. It's a beautiful quality and one that is rarely seen in boxing, and also few and far between in life. Only the very best seem to have that quality, maybe - just maybe - you are the very best."

Davie grinned from ear to ear. Maybe? No question about it.

CHAPTER NINETEEN

PROFESSIONAL OR AMATEUR?

ON MONDAY MORNING, Davie did something he hadn't in a long time: he snoozed the alarm. A lovely weekend of eating and drinking what he fancied had left him a little tired. As the alarm went for the second time, he kissed Aly on the head, got his training stuff together, and headed for the gym.

"Morning, Coach," he says as walks through the door, a few minutes late.

"Davie, see you tomorrow," says the coach.

"What do you mean?"

"You are late, in all the months you've been training with me, you have never been late. Your head is not back in it so I want you to come back when you are ready, like a professional not an amateur."

"Coach, I'm here, come on-"

"Maybe in body, but your mind is elsewhere. Maybe still drinking those cocktails you plastered over social media."

"Coach, please."

"No, Davie, let's try again tomorrow."

"Coach, this makes me really unhappy."

"Well, Davie, happiness is what you put into life, not what you get out of it. How we show up makes who we become. Pressure is a privilege and if you don't want the pressure, hang up your gloves and carry on with life. I gave you three days to relax, and on the fourth day you arrive late, telling me that you forgot where we got to."

"Coach, you are right, I'll see you tomorrow early again."

When Davie gets home and explains to Aly, she tries to defend him. "Aly I appreciate you wanting to defend me, but Coach was right. This is my dream and, for the first time in a long time, I behaved like an amateur. I have to get my head out my backside and be ready. I'm going to spend today thinking, reading, and getting my head and body in the right place."

CHAPTER TWENTY

GIVING BACK

"YOU SEE DAVIE," says Errol, "if you help enough people to get what they want, you will get exactly what you need: time to give back and appreciate how far you have come. Today, we are not going to train. We are going to the homeless shelter and we are going to cook, clean and serve breakfast to people."

Men and women from every background and race, young and old, all turn up at the counter, with only a few coins in their hands. Davie learns that they pay for breakfast, just so they felt a sense of purpose, but the shelter only charges what they can afford. The people were filthy and their clothes were worn out and mismatched. The smell is terrible, and the sadness in their eyes so hard to watch. The odd person smiled and even in their difficult situation seemed to find joy. Davie listens to a few of the stories, some had all fallen on hard times, broken marriages, debt, gambling, drugs, and abuse. It was so difficult to comprehend.

At the end of the morning, they had to scrub the kitchen spotless, mop the floor, and tidy up for tomorrow's guests.

"Bloody hell Coach, this was harder than training. After making over one-hundred breakfasts, I really have a new sense of humility. All these people, the smell, the fear and hunger in their eyes. It really was heart-breaking watching people count out pennies."

As they headed back to the gym, Davie confided in Coach. "You know what, that really did help me appreciate what I have, how blessed I am, and what a lucky SOB I am. I promise you, I will never be late again. This is about discipline, commitment, and perseverance. I have all three and I will not let you down again.

"Sometimes lessons are not always learned in a learning environment," says Coach, "Sometimes, we need to get out of our current situation and see how other people are living and experiencing life.

"I learned a lot about myself today. From seeing how I felt and reacted to the people's stories. It made me realize how lucky I am and that not everybody is as lucky."

CHAPTER TWENTY-ONE

TRAIN HARD, FIGHT EASY

Luck is what happens when preparation meets opportunity.

THE SECOND FIGHT came along against a much more experienced and heavier man.

"Look, we've trained well; you are probably in the best shape of your life. He is more experienced and scarier, so stick to the script, trust the process and we will be fine."

Doubts start to creep into Davie's mind. He felt himself stopping those thoughts in their tracks. This is a time for faith not fear. I have to believe in myself. As he sat in the dressing room, he could hear the crowd singing 'Sweet Caroline' for the fight before his. He remembered what Billy had told him and his mindset began to shift. I am good at this, I am a good fighter.

Then in a flash, Erroll was calling him for the walk out. "How's the head, Davie?"

"It's in a good place Coach, I'm ready and I have given myself a good talking to."

WHAT FELT LIKE only moments later, he was walking back to the changing room. "Wow that was easy," he says to Erroll.

"Train hard, the work is easy," Erroll replies. "Preparation, process, and trust make everything possible. We impressed the crowd tonight, Davie; he had a big following, and you put him on his arse. Remember this, Davie, faith is a muscle that needs to be exercised every day. Don't be afraid to tell the world how great you are."

As the post-match interview came along, he was asked a weird question. "What is your superpower?"

Davie pauses for a second and says, "I think my superpower is belief, success is driven by belief. I believe in me, my team, and our playbook. Eighteen months ago, I was lost and broken. Yet, today I believe anything and everything is possible. Part of the training program included a visit to a local homeless shelter and that helped me refocus, it helped me to put my priorities in the right place. Thank you all for coming tonight, and I look forward to entertaining more in the future."

And that was it. All the training, all the worrying, all the overthinking and it was over in a flash. As he heads home in a taxi, he thinks to himself, sometimes keeping things simple is the only way. KISS: keep it simple stupid!

WHITE BELT THINKING

CHAPTER TWENTY-TWO

GRATITUDE IS THE ANSWER

"WHO CAN YOU thank today, Davie? It's time to show appreciation," says Aly.

"We are very lucky to have each other, to have a happy relationship. You know, Aly, sometimes when you feel helpless, the best thing you can do is find someone else to help. There are times in life we need to be doing more for others than ourselves. And sometimes, we've got to be heartless."

"What do you mean by 'heartless', Davie?"

"You need to use your heart less, be less emotional with your decisions and thinking. Being a heart-centered man is good, but you have to use your head for decisions. I think over the last six months, I had become a little too emotional, worrying too much. Someone told me worrying was planning for a negative future, that's not what I want at all. I want to recharge my energy and be at the top of my game. I really want to work on an attitude of gratitude: this is what will get us through tough times.

So, each day from today I am going to write a gratitude journal, to remind myself who has helped me and to reach out and say thank you. I am going to help as many people as I can to achieve their own dreams. I'm sure in the process, I will get a warm glow from that. I am going to be more present when we are together. Can we agree to get off our phones and start paying more attention to each other?"

"I like that idea," says Aly.

"I am lucky to have you, and I appreciate and love you very much. We will build the greatest life together."

CHAPTER TWENTY-THREE
BE PREPARED FOR ANYTHING

"IT'S NOT HOW good you are, it's how good you can be," Erroll says after training. "Okay, we are on the right path, but how can we take it up a notch to the next level? Who can we attract now to help us get there? We have to go beyond our limited stories and the illusion that our mission is too big, that the challenges we face are insurmountable, or that you don't have enough power to create real change.

"You have the talent, belief, and courage, now it's time to show the world how good we can be. We have had five fights - five wins - people are taking notice of you. Sponsors are knocking at the door. Right now, we are at a crossroads and the next two fights will decide if we get a shot at the British title. Davie, you need to make sure your defense movement is sharp and fast, you need to be too strong for your opponents. Your conditioning and your stamina are unbelievable. No, they are believable. Let's make sure the world is ready for Davie Murphy."

The phone rang and a soft Irish voice says, "You need to come home Davie, Mum is very sick."

Oh boy, here we go again. Davie packs his bags and heads for the airport, this time with Aly beside him. His body is shaking and his legs felt weak.

CHAPTER TWENTY-FOUR

TIME TO REFRAME AND REFOCUS

WHAT DO YOU do when your world is falling apart? Where do you turn next? He sat next to the hospital bed, holding his mum's hand. I think she waited until I got here to say goodbye. Within a few hours, she was gone.

"At least you got to say goodbye this time, Davie," says Margie, his sister.

"True that, sis. It doesn't make it any easier, though, that's not my strong mam I remember, she was frail and weak. I'd hoped she could see me win a title but it must have been her time."

"Davie you sent her all your fights, you helped her be able to give up her working and she spent the end of her life in more comfortable surroundings. I am proud of you as my brother."

"I love you, Margie."

Over the next week, Margie and Davie bonded and Aly was able to get to know hew future sister-in-law. Aly was only able to stay until right after the funeral while Davie was going to stay a bit longer.

Sharing so many lovely stories of his childhood with his sister and slowly sorting through their mum's belongings, Davie found letters and pictures he had sent and written. He was tearful, with fond memories of happy times. They divided up the things they both wanted to keep as mementos. Davie was so sad; he remembered someone once saying it's okay not to be okay, just don't stay there too long. Right now, he was okay with not being okay for a few more days. The Irish food had not been great on his regime and training had taken a back foot. Once the funeral had passed and everything that needed doing was sorted out, he would head back to London. A few years ago, he would not have been able to process all of this, he would have broken down, but here he was now, feeling brave and strong.

"THE FUNERAL WAS a beautiful affair, and the stories and letters people shared will be enough to keep us busy for months. I am going to win the title for Mum," he says to Margie.

"No, Davie, you are going to win it for you, and then dedicate it to Mum."

"Fair enough, I will. It's not how strong you are, it's how strong you can be. One of the guests at the funeral told me this: 'everything you ever want in life sometimes comes gift-wrapped in a problem. Most people do not have the strength or determination to unwrap the problems.' This week you have been my rock and I adore you for that."

This was the first time in his life Davie felt loved by so many others besides Aly but also truly powerful. "Back to London tomorrow to get this show back on the road."

CHAPTER TWENTY-FIVE
IT'S ALL 'NON SENSE'

"NOTHING NEEDS TO make sense," one of his bosses once told him. "Don't let the logic kill the magic."

Here he was back in London, but Aly was nowhere to be found. The flat was cold and he needed to hug her. On the table he found a note: gone back to America, speak when you are back. With everything going on in Ireland, he had been a little distant. But he also had to admit that even before the news about his mum, he had been a bit self-absorbed. He phones her, and she answers.

"It's four in the morning, Davie."

"Oh crap," he replies, "call me when you wake up. I miss you, Aly. I love you and I am sorry for not sticking to our promises we made to each other."

"I love you too. I was feeling a little homesick, so I decided to spend a week with my parents. I'll be back at the weekend. Love ya." And with that, the phone went down.

He decided to pop into the gym. 'Sorry for your loss' came from everyone.

Erroll says, "Boy, you have let yourself go. Time to get back on the plan, Davie, we have a fight in four weeks."

"I just wanted to inhale the smell boss, I'll be back in the gym tomorrow morning at six. 'Non sense' is what got us here. It's time to move from logical to illogical. It's the time to prove everyone wrong."

CHAPTER TWENTY-SIX

NOT THE TIME TO BE AVERAGE

DAVIE WOKE UP early. He began to reflect on his journey so far.

It's time to work out who I am. I have to be the best version of me because everybody else is taken. That sounded like an Instagram post. As we have gone through the phases, he thinks to himself, problems are actually the best things in life.

The more problems you solve, the better your life will be. The only people without problems are no longer here. And as long as you unwrap the problems the gifts will start to appear. The better you get, the bigger problems you need to solve. This was a real learning moment for Davie. I am really waking up with a white belt mentality. This is so powerful. He got changed and headed for the gym.

"Morning sunshine," Erroll greets him. "We have some bad news for you, Davie, your fighter has pulled out and the replacement is a much more experienced boxer. What do you want to do?"

"I don't care who I fight. If I want to be the best, I have to beat the best. Let's watch some videos and train to be able to win."

As the weeks passed, the training intensified. The people he sparred with hurt him, bruised his body and ego, and for the first time in a while he was feeling scared. Aly was back and gave him a good talking-to, but nothing really seemed to get through, so he dialed Taffy.

Taffy starts with, "You have come so far, you seem so open to learning. Remember this, if you think you know it all, you know nothing. If you think you are the cleverest person in the room, you are in the wrong room. You got the sight, height, and the might, but do you have the fight, Davie?"

"I certainly have, I'm just having doubts."

"Why?"

"Well in life we sometimes go through that phase when things are going well, then we start to doubt ourselves."

"It's just a moment to go back to your white-belt thinking, think like a beginner. Here is a question for you, Davie: how long does it take the average person to get a black belt?"

"I don't know. A year, maybe two?"

"No, Davie, it's never."

"Eh?" questions Davie, "how come?"

"Average people don't get black belts. This is your moment to stop being average, stop being so mean to yourself, to stop telling yourself poor quality stories, to stop being your worst critic. It's time to get back to basics and, yes, admire the journey, and enjoy where your feet are. Not focusing on your history, on your future, just be present and available. Will you do that for me?"

"I will, I just let the last couple of weeks get to me."

"You are a human being. You have feelings, it's time to channel them and use them to power you forward, not hold you back. I saw a poem on Instagram today, it went like this:

The only way to know what's possible for you
is to break through the barriers limiting you.
One more step, one more rep, it's up to you
that's what winners do.
– @themotivationalpoet on Instagram

WHITE BELT THINKING

CHAPTER TWENTY-SEVEN

IT'S TIME TO BE FEARLESS, OR JUST FEAR *LESS*

OVER THE NEXT couple of weeks, Davie trained like a champion; it was like a montage from a Rocky film. He was ready. During his first televised fight, he was focused and while he was hurt in the fight, he won on a split decision.

"Are you ready for the European title?" the commentator asks.

"I am ready for the world title," he says and laughs.

"No one has ever achieved this status so quickly, Davie," the commentator continues.

"It may be a short period for you, but for me this is a lifetime in the works. I have the mindset and training camp of a world title winner, all that's missing is the fights. I am ready to push forward and do whatever it takes to win."

In the studio, a few ex-pros debated his style, his energy, and confidence. They believed in him, and this was the extra support he needed to hear. Back in the locker room, Erroll was beaming ear to ear.

"You were fearless tonight or, as you would say,

FEAR LESS. You took some big hits and bounced back. Even when he had you on your arse, you didn't panic."

"I was composed, I felt good and my head was filled with positivity and a winning mentality. I was a white belt thinker from the first bell and nothing negative was getting in my way. Last week, when I spoke to Taffy, he told me about two dogs: a positive dog and a negative dog. Whichever one I fed would get stronger, and every time a negative thought came into my head, I felt that the negative dog was getting stronger. But I just kept feeding the other dog with positivity and love, over and over until it was in control. You see, while you are being positive, it's very hard for negativity to survive. That was the trick tonight."

"Well, it worked, I like that concept, I can even see you sat with your positive dog by your side as I think about it. We got the shot at the title in six weeks, we got your chance to be the best middleweight boxer in Europe and, I believe you can do this."

Aly comes in and hugs him so tight. "Darling, you were tremendous tonight and I love you so much."

Davie feels the love in the room – I need to take a mental photograph of this moment. At the same time, Erroll snaps a picture on his phone of this moment.

CHAPTER TWENTY-EIGHT
THE WORLD LOVES A HERO

THE BIG FIGHT is only a few days away, his opponent is all over social media lambasting Davie as an inexperienced kid. The man is unkind and angry.

Success is a long journey, and you have to jump a lot of hurdles, and pick yourself up time after time, especially after a big setback. Erroll calls Davie into his office.

"Sit down, Davie. Today, we are going to talk about being a HERO."

Davie moves into the room and sits in front of Erroll.

"Okay so H stands for How, E stands for the Event, R stands for React, and O is the Outcome. You see, Davie, how we see the event, and how we react to it is the outcome we get and determines if we end up as a HERO."

Davie nods, seeing what he means.

"At the moment, everyone is throwing mud at you, and you are getting angry. That's a really negative emotion and I don't think the outcome will be positive. Let's go back to Taffy's energy chat, anger is low vibrational energy, it leads to lack of focus, it leads to mistakes and disappointment. That's not what we need now. We need to react to this event with love, positivity, and kindness."

Davie raises his eyebrow.

"Didn't think you would ever hear me say those three words about an opponent, did you? You see, your opponent is scared, he's been waiting for this chance for years and he is angry that a better man might beat him. Not might, will beat him. We have to kill him with kindness, let him lose with love and put him positively on his backside. You need your white belt thinking more than ever. You need to see every punch he throws with clarity, you need to be awake, alive and excited. You need to smile all the way through this fight. Do you understand me, Davie?"

Davie pauses for a moment and replies, "Nothing has ever been so clear in my head, Coach."

Here is a little tip for you, when something happens, before you react, create some space and time. Take some deep breaths to compose yourself, before you respond. How you respond will affect the outcome. You must respond positively. Taking the moment to pause and process will help you to avoid making the wrong choices, leading to a poor outcome. In that space our learning lives.

Life is about the choices we make, and for the avoidance of any doubt, good choices do not always lead to good outcomes. However the more good choices and decisions you make the more your life will be positive. A simple rule you should follow: never get too excited with the wins and never too disappointed with the losses.

Balance is key.

This is your time Davie, NO THING or NO ONE will stop you.

WHITE BELT THINKING

CHAPTER TWENTY-NINE

SEE THE ANGELS AGAIN

AT THE WEIGH in, his opponent tries every tactic in the book to get under Davie's skin. Hurling abuse and threatening to break Davie. Throughout, Davie smiles and says nothing. I will do my talking in the ring. It was the performance of a master with a beginner's mindset.

"HOW DOES IT FEEL to be the European champion, Davie?" asks the Sky Sports commentator?

Davie had done it, he knocked out Lewis within 11 seconds of the 11th round, his angel was back. "It sounds wonderful, Buncie. I want to thank my coaching team, Erroll, Taffy, and everyone at the gym. I did it for my late parents, who I know are sitting front row up in heaven watching me, and my wife-to-be, Aly. I love you Aly. I also want to thank the angel that has been protecting me throughout this journey. I believe in angels and I could not have done it without them."

The crowd roared and cheered, and Erroll and the lads lifted Davie up on to their shoulders.

When they finally put him back down, Coach stands in front with his hands on Davie's shoulders.

"It was a wonderful fight, sunshine," says Coach, "you smiled all the way through, you saw every punch and were combination perfect. We are all so proud of you, Davie, you now are in line for a world title fight. Tonight, your years of planning came true, your vision and stories played out. It was hard in the process, but easy to execute. You were a HERO."

As Davie got back to the locker room, Aly pulls him in and squeezes him so tight. She smiles and gently kisses him on the head. " Let's go celebrate, baby."

CHAPTER THIRTY

REFLECTIONS

A WEEK AFTER the win, Davie and Aly are relaxing in the Lake District, walking, talking, and taking in the fresh air. They reflect on the journey and what they have to do next.

Aly asks, "Who can we meet to get you to the next level, it's now time to find new brains to get you to win the world championship belt."

"I am not going to fight any more, Aly. I am going to retire and focus on building my life with you. I proved my point; I am a champion and I want to retire undefeated. I want to put all my learnings to good use. I am so grateful that we shared this journey together; we went through highs and lows, we went through every emotion known to man. Right now, I want to be the best husband in the world and be a mentor for someone else."

He stops walking and turns to face her.

"Here's what I learned, Aly, winners do things differently: their thinking, language, confidence, belief, and how much they give back. They have to be adaptable. I learned so much from this journey, marginal gains, a beginners mindset, visualizing your future, unshakable belief, constant and never ending improvement. And how important reflection is. We always have to remember who helped us, who we are grateful for, and what's next. I love my life and I love being a life long learner and I will never stop."

If you set the bar so high and jump it, you then wonder why you set it so low.

EPILOGUE

DAVIE DECIDED TO AVOID the obvious route of launching his own clothing range or whisky brand, like the sponsors and many others suggested to him. Instead, he became an ambassador for the RISE Foundation Charity (Recovery in a Safe Environment) and is now working as a mentor with young potential sportspeople whose story is not yet written.

Aly and Davie got married, live in a suburb just outside Atlanta and are expecting their first child. He has not seen the Pyramids yet, and Atlanta has no sea - sometimes just finding the right partner, understanding what you are good at, and being at peace with who you are is enough.

Penny is still searching for love.

Taffy is off looking for the next person to mentor and coach but still keeps in touch with Davie. You see, everyone needs a coach in life.

Erroll and Billy are good friends and are looking for the next Davie too.

I would love to know what you thought of White Belt Thinking! You can write a review with your thoughts at:

- Amazon
- Goodreads
- Facebook

ABOUT THE AUTHOR

SIMON LESLIE IS Chief Executive of Ink, a global media company. He is responsible for delivering high performance and helping leave people better than he finds them. He is married with four boys and spends his time between London, Singapore, and Miami.

He has invested in multiple start-ups and mentors the owners of these companies. Simon coaches high-performance individuals and all the mantras in this book are his, or kindly borrowed from his many mentors and performance coaches over the years.

Having built Ink into a $100m business, the pandemic ravaged the company and its products. Rather than dwelling on the problem, he used his newfound time to write poetry as The Motivational Poet on Instagram and he is currently in the process of rebuilding the company to be even greater and more profitable.

For more information on this and his other books, *No F in Sales*, *Equanimity*, and *Feel Good* visit www.LuckyLeslie.com

NOTES